A Way of Life:
Core Energetics

A Way of Life: Core Energetics

Stuart Black

iUniverse, Inc.
New York Lincoln Shanghai

A Way of Life: Core Energetics

iUniverse, Inc.

For information address:
iUniverse, Inc.
2021 Pine Lake Road, Suite 100
Lincoln, NE 68512
www.iuniverse.com

ISBN: 0-595-32885-7 (pbk)
ISBN: 0-595-66701-5 (cloth)

Printed in the United States of America

To the best, most inspired faculty in the world, at Core Energetics East.

Contents

Acknowledgements

First I want to thank Ruth Fuller, my life partner who has the ability to be there for me no matter what difficulties come her way. I appreciate you more than I can ever say.

The list of those who have helped and inspired me is long. I want to single out Joan Groom, Karyne Wilner, Portland Helmich, and Suzanne Lopez.

Thank you Andrew Black, Rena Black, and Devera Black for your loving and supportive presence in my life.

Thank you Brian Gleason. Your book Mortal Spirit inspired me to finish my book.

I am particularly grateful to John Pierrakos who created so many opportunities for me. And to the students and community that have been my best teachers.

Introduction

I first entered therapy in 1973. My therapist was with a little, tough old lady in her 80s. She asked me why I was there, and I told her the truth. I was married and loved my wife, but I also had a girlfriend whom I loved, and I had recently met a third woman that I was falling in love with, too. She looked up into my eyes and said, "You don't need me; you need a computer."

But I did need her, and so we began talk therapy. I want to be clear that I'm not against talk therapy. Core Energetics has a talk component. People may feel good for a short time after a session in which they had a deep emotional experience, but they will not make any real change in their lives until they understand their reaction to what occurred. They need consciousness or the benefits of the emotional experience will just disappear. Consciousness arises through dialogue. On the other hand, talking and understanding a problem, in my opinion, do not alone produce change. There are many that disagree with me, but I believe humans need energy, emotion, and consciousness to make life changes. We enter a self-searching journey to make changes only to come up against our defenses, which caused our problems in the first place. The defenses end up taking over, and then we do all we can to resist the changes we had said we wanted to make.

I didn't get the computer my therapist recommended until many years later, but I did have emotional experiences in my work with her, and I did make changes. I gave up my girl-friend, and I left my wife. I had no concept of love. If I wanted to have sex with a woman, I believed I had to be in love, and so I kept falling in love. The new woman I had fallen for was in therapy with John Pierrakos, and so I began therapy with him, too. I married this woman, and we had twenty-five won-derful years together.

When I was introduced to Core Energetics, I was a dentist. I sold my business in 1987 after twenty-five years in dental practice. I felt I was doing it for the wrong reasons: money and the prestige of being a doctor. The decision to give it up helped me feel good about myself. I felt that I had integrity and courage and was willing to risk following my heart.

My heart led me to become an actor. I went to acting school full-time for three years and worked as a struggling actor for five more years. I finally came back to Core Energetics when I realized that as an actor I could affect people, but as a Core Energetic practitioner and teacher I could help to change people's lives. I feel I'm doing God's work.

A clear explanation of Core Energetics is difficult if not impossible to find. Over the years, I've struggled through everything written about Core Energetics to find explanations of the basic principles. Finding none, I've been forced to come up with them myself and through my conversations with Dr. John Pierrakos, the founder of Core Energetics.

John died on Feb. 1, 2001. I'm proud to have called him my friend. In my opinion, he was a genius: a gifted, generous man who did God's work. Even though Core Energetics is now taught worldwide in eight countries and is accepted as a major model for any practitioner of body-oriented psychotherapy, the marvel of Pierrakos's work has not yet been explained in writing.

Clearly, students and practitioners need to understand the "magic" behind Core Energetics because it actually makes very logical sense. As world events become increasingly chaotic, however, there's also a need for the human family to develop the necessary tools to live a more fulfilling life.

Why am I the one to explain Core Energetics? I have published articles in the *Core Energetic Journal of Energy and Consciousness*, I've been teaching Core Energetics for twenty-five years and have been the director of the Institute of Core Energetics East for the last sixteen years. I enjoy creating emotional experiences and then teaching Core Energetic principles through these experiences.

The main reason is because I have enormous passion and Eros for this work. I don't just teach Core Energetics, I live it daily. I never intended to teach this work when I started exploring how to find my heart with John Pierrakos in 1975. However, as I became more truthful and willing to be more of who I really am, it became impossible not to have Core Energetics play a major role in my life. Now, it is a way of life for me.

My goal in writing this book is twofold. First, I want it to serve as a teaching manual for students of Core Energetics. Second, I want it to be a tool anyone can use to increase self-confidence and develop more passion and fulfillment in life. I don't mean to imply that such a task is simple. The journey into the self, into who you really are, is difficult and demanding, but it is infinitely worth it.

My hope is the reader will get an understanding of Core Energetics method and how to use it in his or her life immediately, especially how the concept of spirituality and God can change your life.

Chapter 1
Definition

What is Core Energetics?

Spirituality is the foundation of Core Energetics and it's not mentioned enough. John Pierrakos believed that humans are spiritual beings as well as mind-body entities. Contacting Spirit, or God, is the most important tool a Core Energetics practitioner has; in addition, spirituality is the key to living a complete and satisfying life.

Spirituality in Core Energetics means finding your real self: being in truth with yourself, having integrity, contacting your Higher Power, knowing there is more to life than you, and realizing that fulfillment comes from doing your best and doing what is right. This means being with God, trying to do God's will, and doing what God would want even if it doesn't look like what is best for you or your ego at that moment.

This is the purpose of being human in the first place. Our goal in life is to be more of who we really are, which requires a willingness to look into our darkest corners, to know the difficult truths about ourselves.

Fulfillment in life comes from being in touch with what we feel in as many moments as possible. Most of the time we engage in behaviors without knowing how we feel about what we're doing. For example, we may avoid making eye contact with a person of the opposite sex. Every time we see this person, we immediately begin a conversation with someone else. If we intend to know how we're feeling, however, we might discover that our avoidance is a symptom of sexual attraction. Knowing this does not necessitate a change in our behavior; it is the act of knowing what we feel that makes us feel good about ourselves and experience more fulfillment in life because then we are in truth with our feelings, present in the reality of the moment and the excitement of life.

Individual, couples, or group sessions are where the meat of Core Energetics work happens. Still, Pierrakos was very careful to call Core Energetics an evolutionary process rather than a therapy because the concept of therapy seems to be to deal with crises, whereas an evolutionary process is the journey of life. The work of Core Energetics requires that clients want to dissolve their original wounds and evolve into their authentic selves, heart and soul.

Pierrakos birthed Core Energetics in 1972, but Wilhelm Reich, a colleague and disciple of Freud, was the first to observe a connection between the body and psychological/emotional health and dysfunction. Reich observed that his clients' bodies were tensed and distorted as a result of blocked energy. He recognized that this "life energy" was a vital force that flowed into us, through us, and out again into the universe. It's called by many names in different belief systems, but is ulimately the same immortal life-sustaining energy. Reich called it "Orgone" energy.

According to Reich, blocked energy was a response to emotional insults, injuries, wounds, and fears we experienced early in life. He suggested that from birth onward, we "steel" ourselves, holding in rage and other socially unacceptable responses to ensure our survival because we're totally dependent on our earliest caretakers, usually our parents. From the simple but repeated act of holding our breath in fear to the holding of emotions such as rage and grief in the deep and superficial muscles, we build permanent blocks to feelings that were too painful to experience, or so we believed at the time we created the defenses. As a result, we spend our lives locked in a prison of confined, immobilized emotions. The very act of preventing bad feelings also acts to prevent good ones from flowing through us because when we block the flow, we block all flow. Blocked energy does not discriminate. The joys of life become lost to us.

Reich observed that the ages at which these holdings took place actually shaped the body. Through careful study, he could identify not only where his clients held blocked energy but also the psychological character structures these energy blocks revealed.

Core Energetics has devised series of techniques and exercises to fatigue these energy blocks so that the feelings held within them can flow. Once the feelings surface, clients have the opportunity to process them and begin to touch their true selves.

Chapter 2

Characterology

Characterology is the study of character defenses. These defenses are mechanisms we develop to protect ourselves from pain. As helpers, Core Energetic practitioners aim not to dissolve defenses, but to help people become conscious of their existence. That way, they can choose whether they need them or not. Of course, there are times when we need our bodies' defense mechanisms, such as when we're in danger of physical harm. We couldn't and don't want to eliminate them.

why are they so hard to get rid of?

Reasons to study Characterology

There are three main reasons to study the character defenses. By doing so, practitioners will be better able to understand their clients' emotional lives and inner struggles. They will open their hearts to them. Empathy is an ideal emotion for a

Core Energetic practitioner to have. When you empathize, you care about the client and want to help him or her. When your intention is really to help, even if you make a mistake, you will still probably be of help. Studying how the character defenses came about and understanding the distortions and misconceptions of each structure create an empathetic connection between practitioners and their clients.

Another reason to study the character defenses is for the purpose of diagnosis and treatment. Diagnosing clients requires knowing how their injuries, or their wounds, developed. What caused the wound, thereby causing the defense? What is going on emotionally for the client? Treating clients necessitates an understanding of their core and what needs to be done to help them reach it. In treatment, a useful tool is the principle of "charge/discharge," which I will describe shortly.

Finally, the study of the character defenses leads to self-understanding. Practitioners who clearly understand their own issues can be more effective with clients. The more we work on our own struggles, whether we heal them or not, the better we are able to help others with theirs. The more we observe our own journey, the more compassion and insight we have into the journey of others—not from the place of "I'm the teacher; I know the way to help you." We come from a place that identifies with our clients' struggles and therefore touches them on a deeper level.

John Pierrakos and Alexander Lowen left Reich and founded Bioenergetics, one of the first body-oriented therapies. Together, they identified and described five character defenses, which they called "character structures" at the time. Pierrakos and Lowen believed a character defense forms because an emotional wound occurs at a specific developmental time. The infant or child reacts to some type of pain caused by the parental figure. More to the point, the youngster has an energetic reaction that causes the body to form in a very specific way. Because each of us has been wounded, each of us has a character defense, usually more than one.

Character defenses are an amazingly accurate diagnostic tool. Core Energetic practitioners can look at someone's body and know at approximately what age some basic emotional wounds occurred. They can determine where that energy and the unconscious feelings attached to it are held in the body.

When infants don't get the love and/or nurturing they need, a wound is created. However, different souls have different needs. What might wound one might not wound another.

In addition, the older children are when they're first wounded, the more years of love they have had. Later wounds produce adults with more confidence on the material plane. Earlier wounds produce adults with more confidence on the spiritual plane. All of the defenses are formed energetically by age five or six, although they don't take form in the body until puberty. This means you cannot see character defenses in children.

interestingly

When people first experience a Core Energetic session, it may seem like magic because practitioners can know so much of their private lives just by observing their bodies. After diagnosis, a treatment phase follows that might involve some physical exercise or manual manipulation of the body to release blocked energy or repressed feelings into the body so that they have a greater chance to become conscious. Again, the more aware you are of what you feel, the more fulfilled your life will be. You will be present in the moment. Even if it is a painful moment, conscious feelings are liberating on the soul level. In reality, we are feeling something all the time, but we are usually not conscious of what it is. Physically moving energy, or feelings, out of a block is a Core Energetic tool that isn't available in straight verbal therapy.

I do not intend to describe the character defenses. They are described very well in many books, including Lowen's *Language of the Body* and Barbara Brennan's *Light Emerging*. I would, however, like to describe the main dilemma of each person's character defense, the goal of treatment for each structure, and how practitioners can enter a client's energetic system. Practitioners enter the energetic system through the Core Quality, which is called the essence, Higher Self, or God self. Pierrakos believed that we're all spiritual beings at our core and that we're best viewed as our essence and not as a defense against it. When practitioners enter a client's energetic system, they form relationship with that client on a deeper level, a level that enables the client to evolve further on his or her spiritual journey.

Character Defenses

Schizoid: The dilemma of the schizoid is the right to exist on the material plane. The schizoid is the earliest wound. It occurs either prenatally or in the first six months after birth. The infant meets with a hostile environment. This doesn't necessarily mean the parent was hostile, though he or she could have been. It means that the infant, for whatever reason, didn't feel loved and welcomed or that the infant was harmed emotionally before ever knowing he or she was loved. For this infant, the dilemma then becomes "Do I have the right to exist at all?" When there is an emotional threat, these souls turn to God and spirit. They "leave" energetically or go into their minds or wherever they feel safe.

The following is a list of the main diagnostic physical characteristics of the schizoid:

1. *Fear in the eyes.* Because they don't know they are loved or have a right to exist, they live in constant fear and have difficulty finding a safe place to be. The schizoid leaves the material plane and lives in his or her own safe place, usually a fantasy world or a spiritual world.

2. *Disjointed and scattered energy.* The energy of a schizoid person actually leaks out of joints and other places in the body. This is the energetic defense. Again, the purpose of a defense is to protect the individual from a life-endangering threat. As an infant, if the schizoid person had experienced the feelings of not being loved, he or she could not have survived. In Core Energetics, the work of the schizoid is to

contain this energy and bring the feelings attached to it into consciousness in a place of safety and love. How is this done? By grounding the energy. The definition of grounding is being present in the moment, in reality. There is sometimes confusion about grounding. People think it means making contact with the ground. It's true that as Core Energetic practitioners, we often help people ground by doing physical exercises that put them in contact with the ground, like jumping. However, when you're present in the moment, you're grounded. The goal of treatment with schizoid clients is to help them be present in the moment as often as possible, for this is grounding by itself. The work is to try to help them heal their dilemma—to make them conscious of when they are in their defense so they can choose whether they need it or not. When I'm teaching, I like to define grounding as the opposite of the character defense.

If the problem for the schizoid is *not* having a right to exist, then grounding *is* having a right to exist (the opposite of the defense). Balancing checkbooks or arranging dates are useful activities for the schizoid because these are often basic material

bodywork

plane tasks that they have never learned. Furthermore, they often don't feel safe enough to reveal this weakness because they judge themselves; therefore, they can't get any help. They judge themselves for leaving and going to their safe place when they're threatened emotionally. They think there is something wrong with them instead of seeing how leaving was a creative way to save themselves emotionally. Helping them accept this place in themselves and refrain from self-judgment is a major step in their healing.

The Core Quality for the schizoid is their connection to God. The way to connect with them is by helping them make use of their connection to God in daily life. For example, a Core Energetic practitioner might ask, "Why don't you ask God what to do with this problem?"

Oral: The dilemma of the oral is as follows: "I will never have enough. I'm deprived." The defense against the oral wound occurs from three months of age to one year. The oral infant experienced love from a parental figure, but then something happened and it was taken away. This leaves the infant feeling abandoned and trying to get back what he or she lost. The parents were not necessarily "bad." They may not have even abandoned the child. On an emotional level, however, the child experienced the loss of something vital. Having been loved and having lost the security of love leaves them feeling threatened and unsafe. They're never quite sure they're loved.

For the oral, grounding is feeling abundance and generosity, giving to others, and knowing they have enough.

They have two Core Qualities: intelligence (the ability to use their mind) and generosity. Their constant feeling of deprivation makes them unaware of their generosity. When orals perform generous acts, they feel wonderful about themselves because they have connected with their Core. Connecting with their minds is key, though, because they don't trust their emotions. They need to understand things first to trust and take a risk. If you don't connect with their minds, they won't trust you and you won't enter their energetic system.

The following is a list of their main diagnostic physical characteristics:

1. *Pleading in their eyes.* Insatiably, they take your energy from you. They deplete you, making you want to push them away. It's a vicious cycle because this only makes them feel a greater need to get it from you.

2. *Depleted energy.* The oral has the most depleted energetic structure. They get their energy from you. Their bodies are usually thin and long. They've grown away from their hearts. Their necks are long so they can stay in their brilliant minds. The work of the Core Energetic practitioner is to help them find their rage and to mobilize their energy so they can hold it.

Masochist. The dilemma of the masochist is "I won't give anything to you. I'll pretend to comply, but I'll defeat you and me at every turn." The defense against the masochistic wound occurs between the ages of two to three-and-a-half. This is the toilet training age, and many of their issues center around their bodily functions. They are overfed and stuffed from a parent who believes this is a form of loving. A lot of attention was paid to their bowels and their evacuation. Overattention to their digestive tracts produces a soul with a strong wound of humiliation. Survival depended on holding back in any way so they could keep some part of themselves for themselves.

Grounding for masochists is to spend themselves because they hold themselves in. They don't fully exhale, fearing they'll use up their energy. They need to know it is safe to use themselves up and not save some.

Their Core Quality is love, the ability to open their hearts. Seeing this in them helps them feel safe.

The main diagnostic physical characteristics are as follows:

1. *Compact body.* Masochists have a lot of tight, built-up muscle. They are very solid and planted on the ground. Bumping into them is like bumping into a stone wall. Their feet are flat. Their bodies are rectangular blocks. They have short necks because they've pulled their heads into their bodies. To help them, it's necessary to let them know you're both on the same side because anything they do must be for them and not for you. If they think it's for you, they'll comply but defeat any possibility of change. They will feel they gave themselves away.

2. *Held energy.* Masochists are the structure with the most energy, but it is bound up in their muscles so they don't have the use of it. They feel a lot, but refuse to express it.

Psychopath: The dilemma of the psychopath is as follows: "I will never give up control." Whatever happens in any relationship must begin and end with the psychopath being in control. The defense against the psychopathic wound occurs between the ages of three to four-and-a-half. This wound has a lot to do with the relationship with the parent of the opposite sex. The child had a parent who was seductive, who made a false promise. Statements like "You're my little man;" "You're better than your father;" "You know how to do it right" all create a belief in children that they're more than they really are and that they can have something more with the opposite sex parent than is possible. Their unconscious fantasy is to be the partner of the opposite sex parent. The child knows there is a lie in the relationship with the opposite sex parent, but doesn't want to give up the "goodies" of the seduction. This also produces a secondary problem, which is fear of the same-sex parent. If the same-sex parent found out the secret, the child would be killed (or so they believe).

Grounding for the psychopath is to risk being and feeling out of control.

The Core Quality of the psychopath is courage, the ability to take risks. They are the ones who become leaders because of their courage. Others are willing to follow them.

Their main diagnostic physical characteristics are as follows:

1. *Triangular-shaped body.* They are broad in the shoulders and narrow in the feet because their energy exists in the upper part of their bodies. The arches of their feet are high because they try to reach off the ground. Their eyes seem to express paranoia, darting around and on guard. They are not planted on the ground like the masochist. If you bump into them, you'll knock them over. It's difficult for them to trust, and they usually do not feel safe. Their work is to know they are safe and to connect with God.

2. *Upward displaced energy.* Psychopaths are always on the alert for danger and ready to attack. The energy is up in the shoulders and very little in the lower half of their body, so their decisions are mental and not grounded in their body.

Rigid: The dilemma of the rigid is twofold. Their motto is, "I don't feel anything and I must be perfect." They have a lot of feelings, but aren't in touch with them. Therefore, they think they don't feel. No matter what they do, they feel it isn't good enough. The defense against the rigid wound occurs between the ages of four to five-and-a-half. Whereas the psychopathic defense has to do with seduction, the rigid defense has to do with rejection. The rigid was happy with the parent of the opposite sex until the parent told the child he or she was bad and should not engage in some form of pleasurable behavior, like sitting or bouncing on the parent's lap.

Grounding for the rigid is both to feel and to be enough just the way they are.

Their Core Quality is order, the ability to create harmony in their lives and in the world.

The main diagnostic physical characteristics are as follows:

1. *Harmonious body*. These are very beautiful people. They are the performers and models in our society. Working with them is difficult since they can't tell you what they feel. They know something is missing in their lives, but don't know what it is. They are very present on the material plane—the opposite of the schizoid.

2. *Harmonious energy*. The rigid's energy flows and is attractive to see. The problem with the energy flow is that it

narcissism?

jumps over the heart so that contact with feelings is not made.

Chapter 3

The Energetic Concept

When we have any exchange or contact with another, we are dealing with energy, whether we are aware of it or not. We immediately like or dislike someone before uttering a word because an energy has passed between us. Everyone has had an experience of sensing energy at one time or another. Across a room, for example, you might have felt someone looking at you. Some people can even see auras, or energy fields.

Core Energetics is rooted in the belief that an energy flow exists in the body. This energy is in constant motion in a kind of three-dimensional figure eight. For practical purposes, think of the energy as flowing toward the heart. That is, energy below the heart flows up and energy above the heart flows down. In Core Energetics, much of our work centers on feelings. It is simplest to think of feelings as attached to energy; thus, when we talk about energy, we're also talking about feelings.

When energy reaches the heart, it doesn't mean you have love or soft feelings. It means the truth of your feelings can become conscious. You can still prevent the feelings from reaching consciousness, but feelings have a greater chance of becoming conscious when energy reaches the heart.

During an average day, we're constantly experiencing hundreds of feelings. There are many reasons we usually don't know we're feeling. Commonly, we're preoccupied with a task or a goal, but the main reason we're unaware of our feelings is that we prefer not to make them conscious, particularly aggressive or sexual feelings. An unconscious mechanism within us says, "Oh, I feel sexual. I don't want to deal with that. It's too threatening, go away." This unconscious statement activates our defense mechanisms, keeping our feelings unconscious.

Energetically, the body's defense system produces blocks and leaks. Blocks and leaks are very important aspects of Core Energetics because they are used as diagnostic and treatment tools.

A block is a muscle that stays in a contracted state for the purpose of preventing feelings from reaching consciousness. Blocks are located all over the body. Once you're familiar with them, you can obtain information about people. This is part of the "magic" of Core Energetics.

There are two types of energy in the body. The first type is the energy flow; the other is the energy located in the block, which holds back and prevents the flow. To prevent energy from circulating, the energy in the block must be even greater than the energy flow. Actually, there is only one energy supply—it is just simpler to separate these energies into two camps. The energy we work with in Core Energetics is the one that holds back the flow.

You or someone you know might have had the experience of being first tired and weak, later becoming exhausted, and finally emerging less tired because you engaged in some kind of physical movement. This happens in a Core Energetic session when a client hits an object with a foam bat, for example. The shift happens when we stop wasting energy by holding it down. That is, the energy in the block that was holding down the flow became exhausted. If we're no longer using up energy, more energy is actually available to us as a result, and then, the extra energy that is released makes us feel even more alive.

Diagnosis

You can diagnose movement or nonmovement of energy in three ways:

1. Vision: It's possible to see those muscles that stay in a contracted state, preventing energy flow.

2. Touch: With touch, you can feel a muscle's tightness and its movement or nonmovement of energy.

3. Sensing: You can sense the movement or nonmovement of energy.

This is not as difficult as it may sound. First, adopt a posture so that your own body is open and not blocked. Stand with feet shoulder-width apart and toes pointing straight ahead. If the toes are open, pointing outward from the body, the buttocks tighten and cut off all available energy supply below the waist. Try opening and closing your toes while standing and note the differences yourself. Next, bend your knees slightly or the energy will become blocked there. Bring your pelvis forward. Open the palms of your hands and direct them toward the person's body. You can receive and/or send energy from this posture. The energy runs from the left hand to the right hand across your chest. This stance is like an energy meter and is surprisingly accurate.

The purpose of this posture is to open yourself so that you are available to receive information from the client. You can't receive it with your mind. It comes through the body from God. Perceiving the energy supply tells you where people are unconsciously holding feelings they don't want to confront.

Treatment

Once you discover the energy supply, the next step is helping clients feel safe enough to deal with the unconscious feelings. You cannot simply send them into the body. People must be emotionally ready to face them and must be in a secure environment with someone they trust.

Principle of Charge/Discharge

The main technique for releasing the held energy into the body (not out of the body where feelings will be lost) is something I call charge/discharge. This is not the principle of charge/discharge Reich described in his book *Function of the*

Orgasm. The charge I'm talking about puts even more pressure on the muscle that is preventing the flow of energy and causing the block. A strong physical movement creates the charge. For example, if the energy is held in the shoulders (one of the most common places to hold energy), the client might hit a large foam cube with a foam bat or a tennis racket. Alternatively, the client might punch the cube. This action puts pressure on the energy held in the shoulders, creating a "charge." The charge does not cause the client to get in touch with his or her feelings, however.

Feelings can be contacted holding a stationary position, such as bent over with a stretch behind the knees or perhaps standing with the knees slightly bent. This posture creates a "discharge," which is a release of the energy (or feelings). The goal is to release the feelings into the body. Doing so gives clients the greatest opportunity to make their feelings conscious. Sometimes, clients will shake their hands or feet and literally throw the feelings out of their bodies. This action also creates a discharge, but it is a discharge that expels the feelings from the body, preventing them from reaching consciousness. It is important to note that hitting, kicking, and punching are not about expressing aggression or anger in Core Energetics.

Rather, performing these actions puts pressure on those muscles that are preventing the body's flow of energy. It is a misconception that Core Energetics is about expressing anger or hostility. The act of hitting may bring up feelings of anger, but clients do not need to be angry to engage in the physical act of hitting.

Another way the body prevents energy from becoming conscious is with a leak. A leak produces an effect similar to that of a block. Leaks, which are most often connected to the schizoid dilemma, are an energetic hole that looks like a deep depression in the muscle. Energy pours out of the body from this hole to prevent it from continuing its journey toward the heart, where consciousness resides.

Core Energetics aims to get energy flowing freely within the body. It's important to note that energy can also flow beyond the body and affect others. The next time you're at a party, try sending some loving energy to a friend across the room and see if your friend responds, even if he or she isn't looking at you.

Chapter 4

Contact

We all struggle in our lives with how to make contact with others, how to develop a connection, how to touch or be touched by someone. In Core Energetics, we view contact on a spectrum that contains degrees of intimacy. We don't want intimacy with everyone. We want intimacy with those we care most about, such as our life partners or best friends.

It is helpful to divide intimacy into two parts that are opposite sides of the same coin. The first part is the willingness to reveal yourself to another, to let someone see as much of who you really are as possible. The more you are willing to open yourself to another, the more intimacy you will have in your relationship, the closer you will feel. You will reveal more of yourself to some people than to others, and that is perfectly appropriate. It is up to you to decide with whom and to what degree you wish to be intimate.

The other half of intimacy is the willingness to take the other in, to have the intention to see someone for who he or she truly is. Genuine intimacy necessitates seeing people not as you want them to be, but how they really are. In a relationship, if you can open yourself to your partners, friends, or relatives and also accept them for who they are, you are on your way to experiencing bliss.

Core Energetics seeks to help individuals have a more fulfilling life, and one of the most important elements in a fulfilling life is in our ability to make contact with others. When we're able to reveal our true selves to others as well as take them in, we have one of the main tools for intimacy.

seeing & accepting people as they are

Mask, Lower Self, Higher Self

The initial concept of the mask, lower self, and higher self came from Eva Pierrakos, the wife of John Pierrakos. Eva was a medium and channeled wisdom from an entity called the "Guide." The mask, lower self, and higher self are a description of the human personality. Understanding these facets of ourselves helps us accept ourselves more. When we make contact with them, we become more truthful about whom we really are. We're able to make contact with others on a deeper level.

Much of the work in Core Energetics relates to the mask, the lower self, and the higher self. Most people live most of the time in their masks. The mask is a socially acceptable face that is also acceptable to the person "wearing" it. Its function is to hide the selfish, self-serving feelings of the lower self. Most people don't reveal their lower selves because they fear the negative reactions of others. A good example of a lower self-statement is, "I don't care about you or what you want. I just want what I want right now, so get out of my way or I'll take it from you." Most of the work we do in Core Energetics helps people out of their masks and into their lower selves.

In the mask, it is not possible to make any change. People in their masks blame and judge; they don't take any responsibility for their actions or behavior. The lower self, however, owns up to unpleasant feelings and selfish desires. Therefore, change is possible. When we have people hit an object with a foam bat to energize negative feelings in Core Energetics, the purpose is to pull them out of their masks and into their lower selves. As much as the lower self is cruel and selfish, it also represents a truthful place. The client feels relief and satisfaction after expressing it. Creativity, positive aggression, sexuality, and passion are all positive energies that have gotten trapped and distorted by the lower self.

People fear expressing their lower selves for two main reasons. First, they don't want others or even themselves to know they possess selfish and cruel qualities. Second, they find pleasure in the aggression, albeit negative pleasure. This kind of pleasure is similar to passion. The person doesn't know the difference between this "negative" feeling and a "positive" one—they just know there's something they don't want to lose. Once they give up these distortions and misconceptions, they will feel much greater pleasure because it will be coming from their inner truth without guilt.

The higher self is the "Core" of Core Energetics. It is the God self, the inner wisdom, integrity. They are all the same. There are misconceptions about the higher self, too. One misconception is that you need to do something to reach it. Actually, the higher self emerges when you are in truth. Consequently, exposing the lower self allows the higher self to manifest effortlessly. The higher self does not always hold heartfelt, loving feelings; rather, it holds the feelings of truth. It's different from the lower self in that it wants to do what is right. The higher self is not selfish. In the higher self, there are no doubts; it is not difficult to say or do anything. You just are. There is no fear, no need to be more than you are. There is no need to get anything from others.

You cannot move from the mask to the higher self without going through the lower self. If you try to do this, you will merely acquire another mask, a mask of the higher self, but not the higher self. Not trusting it to emerge organically, you will have only the pretense of higher-self qualities.

Chapter 5

Community

It took me a long time to realize that the guiding passion in my life and the major contribution I have to make to Core Energetics—and to the world—centers on the power of community. I believe all of us are searching for community. We may not describe it that way, but we long to belong, to feel safe, and to search with others on a similar path. The search, of course, is really a search for God. ?

Guidance

Searching for that sense of contentment and inner peace, you have more resources than you realize. You can use Guidance to make contact with your higher self. This is your place of inner truth, knowledge, and safety. When you rely on

Guidance, the wisdom that emerges can be profound. This source of wisdom is always available to you.

There are different ways to make use of Guidance. Meditation is one way, of course, but you can also use the written word. Remember that you're beginning to establish a relationship with Guidance. Just as in an intimate relationship, you need to reveal yourself genuinely and take the other in. Write down a question, something very specific that cannot be answered satisfactorily with the rational mind. As you write the question, then write the answer. Write it without thinking about what you're writing. Don't let the words go through your mind. You might not even know what you have written until you read it. It may even come out as gibberish. Your question might be, "Why does my partner always keep me waiting and isn't considerate enough of me?"

Your intention must genuinely be to want to know the truth, not to build a case against the other. The answer to a question like this—if you're open to hearing the truth—would in some way help you look into yourself. It wouldn't highlight what your partner is doing wrong. An answer might be, "What you need to look at is why waiting brings up these feelings of not being considered." When you first open up the channel to this Guidance, your questions may need to be about trusting it. You might have questions like, "Where does this Guidance really come from?" "Will this really work?" "I don't even really believe in God or spirits, so how can this work?" "What is your name?"

The conscious intention to seek help from the Spirit World instantly changes things. It shows a desire to know the truth, not to be right or to satisfy your ego or gain some advantage over another. This act creates an immediate connection to God. I believe the Spirit World is part of our community and is always available to us. We have only to ask. It is up to us to make the contact, but it must be from a genuine place. Otherwise, the answer will come from your mind and not from eternal wisdom.

The act of using Guidance immediately produces inner peace. Asking to know God's way instead of your way is a very spiritual act. There is always an answer from Spirit if the contact is sincere. If answers don't come, it's because the ego is in the way or because the response is misinterpreted.

Energetic Concept of God

If we believe that energy flows within us, then it isn't so hard to believe that it can also flow beyond our physical bodies. If this is so, a group of people can send loving energy into the middle of a room. It's possible to feel the presence of this energy in the room, and one or all of us can take some of it to help us feel loved and supported. Once we see that this loving energy exists everywhere, whether we have contributed to it or not, we are on our way to understanding the energetic concept of God. God is a loving energy available to us anytime we choose to call upon it.

I notice in my teaching that there is a hunger for contact with God. People want to know how to talk to God, use God in their work with others, and bring God into all aspects of their lives. Pierrakos described spirituality as all the aspects of love. The "Core" of Core Energetics is not human energy, the body, or consciousness (although these are all important); it is God, or all the aspects of love.

The Spirit World

One way to tap into Guidance is to contact the Spirit World, where entities whose purpose is to help humans on their journey to God exist.

The whole notion of spirits surfaced in my life when my mother died in 1985. I felt more alone than I had ever felt before. I knew there were people who loved me, but the person who had always been there for me unconditionally was gone. I sunk into a depression. I had been struggling to make contact with God because I was in need of wisdom and peace. I was moderately successful receiving answers to questions that I knew I couldn't have arrived at on my own. Coming from Source, which I think of as Spirit, I was beginning to contact angels or emissaries of God. These are souls who've finished their journey on the earth plane. Their task is to help humans find their truth and therefore their way back to God.

One day when I was feeling more deeply alone than ever before, I felt the physical presence of four angels, three male and one female, holding and comforting me. This may sound preposterous, but after many years I can confidently say that it is not. It's taken me a long time to develop the courage to speak of this experience, but as I get more comfortable in my own truth it gets easier. Even though I may still be lonely at times, I know on the deepest level that I'm never really alone.

Community in Core Energetics

The realization that I had a team of spirits who loved and supported each other and me led me to the idea of teaching and working with Core Energetic principles in teams. Teams are groups of people organized for a particular purpose. In Core Energetics, the purpose is to serve the client. To create a community of faculty and students, Core Energetics has a practice model that begins with a four-day residential retreat.

Typically, the ratio is three Core Energetic practitioners to one client. Thus, five clients would require five teams of three practitioners each (fifteen practitioners in all). Each client has individual sessions with these three practitioners. In addition, the five clients participate in a group with the fifteen practitioners and with my life partner, Ruth, and me. Thus, there is the community of the twenty-two of us as well as the practitioner and client communities. The five clients form a community of receivers, and the practitioners form a community of givers. In the end, the line between the givers and the receivers becomes blurred because true giving is receiving and true receiving is giving. Ruth and I help practitioners deal with their issues of competition and come to a loving and trusting place with one other.

I have a preference for teams of three people. Such teams have many wonderful qualities even though it's very challenging for three people to get along. Two people can compromise, and four can pair up and support each other. Three people have a struggle. They fight and compete; someone is always left out. In short, teams of three are a microcosm for the difficulties we experience in life. In Core Energetic groups, we deal with these difficulties with the goal of finding the truth and aligning with God. When teams deal with their competitive issues, they come to a unifying place. The task of a team member is to support the other two members, so there are always two people supporting one individual. Because of this, they can model care and concern for each other when they work with clients, as they have created a safe environment where they are free to be themselves. Clients then feel safe to journey deeper than they would ordinarily.

Working on a team while serving a client, practitioners inevitably get stuck, and this is a perfect teaching opportunity. Getting stuck simply means that the practitioners don't know what to do. They feel lost or incompetent. The usual response when someone is stuck is either to show how much smarter you are by judging or to come to a team member's rescue by helping. In a Core Energetic session with a team of three practitioners and one client, members of the team learn to send the "stuck" person love. They wish him or her well. They let the team member know he or she has their support. The stuck person's inspiration comes back more often than not.

As each team of three practitioners unifies, they can then unify with other teams in the same way their team unified by dealing with their competitiveness and by freeing up their love for each other. The whole community of five teams can then bond as one.

The other team we use at Core Energetics East is a teaching team. This is a team of eight teachers, teaching a class of twenty to twenty-five people. The eight teachers prepare the classes together and support each other. Only three teachers are in the class at the same time, as more than that would overwhelm the class. The teachers rotate so each of them gets a turn. The purpose of team teaching is that teachers can share not only their responsibilities, but also their excitement with each other. Furthermore, the class has the chance to experience the unity and safety teams can engender, which helps students learn on a very deep level.

This team concept in Core Energetics is new to teaching and to client work. It requires deep personal process work from team participants. They must be committed to taking their own journey.

Leadership

Leadership is a very important aspect of any community. There is a difference between being a leader and being an authority figure. While leaders serve their followers, authority figures serve themselves.

In my team model for teaching students of Core Energetics, the first task is choosing a leader. Every team must have a leader. A leader is not a leader unless he or she claims it. The team cannot say, "I think you should be the leader." The leader must say, "I want to be the leader." The others must say, "I'm willing to follow you." The process of becoming a follower is just as important as the process of becoming the leader.

The main job of a leader is to serve. The leader's job is not to do everything or to order others to do everything, but to serve the needs of the followers. You lead as long as you have something to give that is needed by the others. They, as followers, choose to give over to you, not because you are always right or smarter, but because they trust you to do what is in their best interests.

To form a real community, people must bond with each other. For that to happen, an environment of trust and safety that allows people to be themselves must exist. Over twenty-four years of conducting Core Energetic groups, I discovered that it was very difficult to bond a group of more than ten people. It could take months or even years. A group of three people, however, could bond in a day or even a few hours. They could not only bond, but also experience unity, the state of being one. In unity, your pain is my pain; your pleasure is my pleasure.

As I've said, the purpose of being human is to discover who we really are, to become our real selves. I call this process a journey to God. When you reach a certain place in your own development, it is time to take this journey with another person, which is infinitely more difficult and infinitely more rewarding. This journey to God is the basis of all intimate relationships. I don't think people make any major life changes without believing that life is about more than accumulation on the material plane. It's about living from your integrity— living for what your heart knows is right, which is God.

It is important to note that when you are feeling seen and feel wonderful in a supportive and loving community, this is the "real world." The world we usually live in and go back to is the fake world. Our task in Core Energetics is to know we carry this real world with us and to make it manifest.

Chapter 6
Steps of a Session

There are several things that make a Core Energetic session different from other therapy sessions. The differences are listed subsequently as steps. However, the most important aspect of a session and the most important thing to accomplish in a session are establishing a relationship with the client. There must be a relationship of trust that allows the client to feel safe enough to journey as deeply as possible. The relationship is primary; everything else is always secondary to it. This relationship is also known as establishing the transference.

Contrary to conventional thought, transference is a positive thing. You need it to accomplish the work. Eliminating transference is impossible and unproductive. Clients believe you have skills that can help them, and they may believe you're special, even more special than you really are. These beliefs enable them to journey more deeply. If you were equal to them, why would they need to come to you for help? Of course, you must not abuse the transference and believe you're superior. Instead, you must use their trust to help them go to the deepest place possible. The following steps are instructions for a practitioner of Core Energetics, but they are also valuable for clients looking to understand the reasons for these procedures in sessions.

Step 1. First, gather information by looking at the body. This is easier if the client removes some outer clothes. Clearly, removing clothing is a very sensitive act. It can take many months for clients to feel comfortable enough to remove pieces of clothing, and they may never do it all. This must be respected. Clients should never be observed in their underwear. They should wear shorts or bathing suits. The parts of the body that you want to see are the neck, eyes, shoulders, chest, belly, waist, knees, feet, and knees, elbows, wrists, and ankle joints. Seeing these parts allows you to observe where energy is blocked or leaking; it also allows you to see where the energy supply is. Noticing where energy is present and where it's nonexistent is important because it tells you where to begin the physical work of getting energy into the body so the client has a greater opportunity to make unconscious feelings conscious. For instance, if you see tightly bound muscles in the client's shoulders, that means there's a surplus of energy there. You'll want the client to do something to release that energy into the body. Observation of the body is a powerful tool for Core Energetic practitioners.

It is possible to do very important work around why the client doesn't want to take off his or her clothes, if this is the case. Clients need to remove clothing in privacy, and their vulnerability needs to be honored.

Intention

Step 2. The second step is to attune. That means to set an intention for what you would like to accomplish in the session and to align with truth and with God. The attunement is a type of prayer that emphasizes the important role God plays in this work. At the beginning of a session, practitioners and clients can say a prayer together that sets an intention for the session. Practitioners can say something like, "Please God help me give my best to Jim without needing anything back." Being there for clients without needing them to produce anything is not a simple task. What's required is the intention and the desire to open the heart and be there for the client. It's important for practitioners to trust that their skills and knowledge will be there when they need them and focus instead on their hearts.

Setting this kind of intention cannot only have a profound effect on a Core Energetic session, but the whole concept of intention can also have a profound effect on your life. It can actually produce an immediate sense of peace and satisfaction. It's a simple principle, but difficult to incorporate into everyday life.

An intention is your true, unconscious motive. It's the real reason you're doing something, even though you may not know it. A positive intention yields unity with yourself and with others. It is the flow of life. A negative intention yields separation from yourself and from others. It is motivated by pride, self-will, and fear.

Creating a positive intention requires the following:

A. Consciousness: Want to know the intent of all your actions. Being sweet isn't necessarily a positive thing. It can be a mask, a cover for a negative intent. Wanting to know your intent is a step toward consciousness. When you know your intent, you have accomplished consciousness.

B. Acceptance: Accept it if you have a negative intent. This is a big deal. After the intent becomes conscious, you might think it's gone. That means you haven't accepted it. You can't change anything if you haven't accepted it. You have to live in it for awhile. See how it feels to admit it. This is where your lower self resides. Find the pleasure here. You can't change your lower self, but you can change your intention. If you can find the misconception, then you can keep the pleasure. You may fear that you'll have to give up pleasure. What you give up, actually, is the negative attachment to the pleasure. (My subsequent example makes these concepts of pleasure and misconception clear).

C. Desire to have a positive intent and to give up the negative intent.

D. Pray for help from God. Ask to align with this desire. Prayer is essential. You may need to pray for everything: consciousness, acceptance, the desire for a positive intent, and the relinquishing of the negative intent.

When I first started to teach, for example, I got a lot of very positive feedback. Still, I didn't feel good at the end of the day. I wasn't satisfied; something was missing. It took me a long time to reach this awareness. Finally, I realized I might have a negative intent. This was step "A" (consciousness), noted earlier.

I discovered that I wanted my students to think I was wonderful, and I didn't really care how much they learned from me. This was a very painful observation for me. It didn't fit my image of myself, so I could understand that I hadn't realized it sooner. Clearly, I didn't want to accept this about myself. What I did was say, "Now that I've seen this, it doesn't exist anymore." That is not accepting it. I needed to live in and accept the pain of selfishness. This was the aforementioned step "B" (acceptance).

Finally as I went further and I looked for the pleasure in my negative intent, I realized it came from having the students believe I was great. This was clearly a misconception. The real pleasure comes from giving my best, from sharing what I know and feeling God smiling on me. From this place, I was able to pray for a positive intent and real pleasure (steps C & D mentioned earlier).

To give because I want you to admire me is a way of taking from you. To give to you because I care is really giving to you, and it leaves me feeling good in the end. When there is a negative intent, you feel bad even when there is a positive response.

Step 3. While the first step is about being able to look at the client's body, the third step is about actually looking at the body. It is as difficult to look at someone's body as it is to have someone look at your body. The important thing is to really look. Let the client watch you look and deal with how he or she feels about your looking. The most important part of this step is not what you see, but how you feel about what you see. If you only stay with what you see, you become clinical. You may be accurate, but you separate yourself from the client and make the environment unsafe. Allowing yourself to be in touch with how you feel—whether you have feelings of empathy, vulnerability, sexuality, or even anger—brings you into the session emotionally and allows you to be intimate with the client.

From this intimate place, all kinds of magic can happen. If you are feeling anger or attraction toward the client, it is important to know this. Keeping it unconscious causes you to behave or speak from a place other than your heart and therefore does not deepen the client's journey. The client does not need to know you are angry. In my opinion, the best way to deal with these feelings is to pray. Ask God to let you keep your feelings, but use them in the client's best interests. Ask that you not want anything for yourself. Wanting anything for yourself is countertransference and needs to be avoided. In addition to being in touch with what you are feeling, you must be willing to allow what you are feeling to show, especially if it is compassion or tenderness. The client will sense this energetically and feel even safer.

Step 4. The next step is to help the client move his or her energy. Moving energy is the purpose of all Core Energetic techniques. What does this really mean? Releasing unconscious feelings into the body and helping the client analyze them is a major contribution of Core Energetics. You want to do this as early in the session as possible. I strongly recommend that physical, energetic work be done before a lot of conceptual talking, perhaps within the first five to ten minutes of the session. Physical work enables more feelings to be present, and there is a greater chance for them to become conscious. Moreover, clients will be able to go deeper in their search, and the conversation will be more meaningful. If the client doesn't move energy until the latter part of the session, there isn't enough time to deal with the issues that arise.

Step 5. The last step of the session is consciousness. If clients have an emotional experience without any consciousness, there will not be any change. They need to look at and understand the meaning of the feelings that have come up. This will help them discover their Real Selves, or God.

Your Real Self is who you really are. We put a lot of effort into being more or less than we really are, into being better or worse than others. When you can be who you are with the knowledge that you have without pretending to know more than you do, you'll have confidence in yourself. You will feel good and will have more freedom than you have ever had.

Chapter 7

Practical Aspects of a
Core Energetic Group

My passion for groups started in 1976 when I was a member of a group led by John Pierrakos, who cast his magic spell on me. His ability to receive whatever came toward him and remain confrontive and loving at the same time was a great model for me. I wanted more, so I became a student at the Institute of the New Age, which was a precursor of the Institute of Core Energetics. Eventually, I did workshops wherever I could, workshops at the Association of Humanistic Psychology and the Open Center. I led groups for dentists. I led groups at the Phoenicia Pathwork Center and finally at the Institute of Core Energetics.

More than any other therapeutic form, I think groups present individuals with the greatest potential for change. Using the energy of others in the group to affect the person doing the work is a wonderfully exciting experience. The purpose of a group is to create an environment where people can explore their deepest life struggles, where they can feel seen and safe while healing the distortions and misconceptions that prevent them from finding fulfillment in life. The effects of being in a group include acquiring the capacity for intimacy and making a connection to something beyond the self, such as God or Inner Truth.

Core Energetics involves using yourself and your present-moment feelings. I'm going to present a series of different circumstances where group leaders, both those who are teaching students of Core Energetics and those who are leading Core Energetic groups for the general public, get into trouble or behave in a way that hinders the group's development. I'll also present some possible ways out of these situations.

The Core Energetic Group

What makes a Core Energetic group different from any other group? There are three main elements in a Core Energetic group. Actually, there are dozens of elements, but there are three that are especially pertinent here.

1. First, there is the energy component. There is an energy supply in the body that is not being used because it is blocked, armored, or leaks out of the body. This is a major concept in Core Energetics and is the origin of the charge/discharge principle, which is used to make this energy available in the body. It is important to reiterate that the energy is released *into* the body so the feelings can emerge; the energy must not be thrown out of the body. This kind of energy work is a major difference between a Core Energetic group and other types of self-development groups. We focus on the energy of the person working in the group as well as the energy of the group members.

2. The next major difference is that we observe and use the body for diagnosis and treatment. Because this is a central part of Core Energetics, I want to clear up some basic misconceptions about looking at bodies. I discussed this in chapter six, but reiterate it here because looking at the body with others present (in a group) is an even greater risk for the client. Taking off clothes naturally brings up feelings of vulnerability. This vulnerability may be as important as anything you will diagnose. The actual act of undressing and dressing should be private. Again, women

should wear shorts and a sports bra; men can wear shorts. This attire allows you to see enough of the body to observe the major blocks. When the client appears, he or she should be taken in and honored for his or her courage and vulnerability. It is at this point that you need to take at least five minutes to look at the body. Be direct and tell the client why you are looking. Acknowledge the client's feelings and answer any questions that arise. You are looking not only to diagnose, but also to be aware of how you feel about what you see. The art of Core Energetics involves bringing your awareness of yourself into the work instead of pushing it away to rise above it. The act of looking at the client's body and what that brings up could be the entire work of the whole group.

3. The third element that distinguishes a Core Energetic group is the spiritual conviction that true healing and change only occurs when we make contact with our inner "Core." This is our God self, our Truth, our Higher Self, our Inner Wisdom, our Love, our Integrity. In the end, all of these things are the same. They are our search for wisdom beyond our minds. The desire for this contact adds

an important dimension to Core Energetics, whether there is any contact with the God self or not.

Differences Between Individual and Group Sessions

There is a world of difference between individual sessions and group sessions in Core Energetics. The difference begins with the attention and energy you give to the client. In an individual session, the client gets 100 percent of your attention. In a group of either students or lay people, the client should not get more than 50 percent of your attention. This is an area where group leaders can hinder the development of the group. You must give at least equal energy, if not more, to the members of the group. If you don't, they will become bored, which means they will not be involved in what is going on. That is why, for want of a better word, there is what I call the "entertainment" factor in a group. The best form of entertainment is when there are strong emotions involved in the "performance," and the audience (the members of the group) share and identify with the experience of the "performer."

I don't mean to imply in any way that a group session is a performance. It must be a true journey to whatever depth the person doing the work is capable of reaching at the moment. However, others must be involved and not excluded. If you lead a group session with a soft, intimate voice, you kill the energy. Of course, you want to establish intimacy with the person doing the work, but the group must be included in that intimacy.

While you might start an individual session with physical work to help ground the client, it's even more important that every group begin with Core Energetic exercises. The purpose of the exercises is to put a "charge" on the energy supply. Exercises could include stretching, jumping, or even dancing. Everyone, including the leader, has come from a different place and brings different energy to the group, whether it's the stress of the day or even the pressure of trying to arrive on time. Getting your energy flowing together helps to bring everyone into the moment and makes all the participants more available to enter the group process. It is important to bring everyone into the same moment so that mutual energy exists for the group to use. That is what grounding really is: being in the moment.

The transference group members make to a group leader is different from the transference an individual client makes to a

Core Energetic practitioner or to a therapist. In an individual session, the client hears opinions and interpretations from the practitioner and takes them in, while at the same time resisting the practitioner's "authority figure" role with a "What do you know?" or "Of course, *you* can say that" type of attitude. In a group, feedback can come from peers, who ideally don't have any stake in anything other than speaking their truth as they identify with the experience. The impact of this type of feedback can be much greater on the client; therefore, the potential for change is also much greater. Group leaders can actually hinder the group's development by drawing too much of the focus. The leader's goal is to have the members of the group give as much feedback to the client as possible. In an ideal group, the members are not even aware of the direction and the form the leader is creating. Much of the effect of the work comes from the client going to an emotional edge, feeling the danger and threat present in taking a risk, and being able to feel the support and identification from other members of the group.

In addition, in group sessions, members can be used to assist and touch the client. This is especially beneficial. The most important reason is that members of the group become involved and bring their energy into the work. A major goal of a group session is to use the energy of the group to take the work further and deeper than would otherwise be possible. If the work is tender and the client's heart is opened, having group members who feel so moved make a pile of hands on the client's heart can have a powerful impact on the client while also helping to bond the group. Please note that I said, "members of the group who feel so moved." It is important not to require anyone to touch or support someone else. It must be okay not to do so. For the support to have an effect, it must be real. Anytime you ask someone in the group, or the group as a whole, to do something, you must ask permission. If you don't, resentment will build, and the work will begin to lack authenticity.

The way leaders use themselves in a group is of great importance. Leaders can make choices to reveal themselves much more than they would in individual sessions. It does not serve the group for the leader to create an air of always knowing what to do. If you are the group leader, revealing doubts and allowing the negativity of the group members to come toward you are great gifts to the group. The more human you are, the more you show integrity and courage.

This is not only modeling behavior, but it also creates safety and trust in the group. The greatest sign of competence is the willingness not to know. When you reveal your imperfections, you are free to be yourself in the group. Therefore, take risks and make mistakes. That's right, make mistakes. Being careful of mistakes blocks creativity and prevents spontaneity and flow. If your intent is to give your best, there is no such thing as a mistake, only another opportunity to discover something. What a gift it is to the group to admit you are wrong or sorry for something you did.

The most important thing to do when negativity comes toward you is simply to receive it and get beaten to death if that's what it takes. (Of course, I'm speaking figuratively. Members should use a foam bat or punch a pillow. You should never risk being hurt). After this, admire the courage it took for the individual to give that negativity to you. You don't have to let the person know you admire him or her (although it's useful if you can). Just contacting that place in yourself will give the individual a great deal because he or she will feel the positive energy that comes from you. The individual will know you're on his or her side. Avoid the fear that you're going to be harmed as well as the need to defend and protect yourself from being found "incompetent."

The rule that I would suggest is to consider that whatever you do as the leader needs to serve the best interests of the members of the group first, the individual who is working second, and yourself not at all. As soon as you do something for yourself, it is an abuse. It represents countertransference, and you need to work on it in supervision. This is not to say that you don't get a lot of personal needs met in a group, particularly the need to be appreciated, respected, and even admired. These come as fringe benefits of having given of yourself for the benefit of the group.

In a group you can and *should* use physical exercises and movement even more than in a private session, because it involves the whole group more and moves the energy within the body. This is a lot of what Core Energetics is all about. If energy can move within the body, it can also move beyond the body and reach someone else's body. This is an important concept because it means that the energy of the members of the group can also affect the person working at the moment. Remember that, for all practical purposes, "energy" and feelings are the same. My point is that you need to minimize the verbal and increase the experiential in a group, including as many members of the group as possible. The experience then remains in the moment and you can say, "See, that's what I'm talking about." You want the energy (feelings) of the person working to affect the members of the group so they will bring their energy (feelings) to the work and help it go deeper.

The number of people affected intensifies the group experience. On the other hand, the opposite is also true: if, as the leader, you diminish the feelings of the group members, you withdraw energy from the group. If you stay on the mental, conceptual level, group members will not feel connected to the work, and they will "leave" the group emotionally. Their minds will wander; they'll feel like they're someplace else. When this happens, it becomes difficult, if not impossible, for important work to occur.

Creating a Safe Environment

In groups you can "push" the work more than you can in individual sessions. Creating a situation where members of the group can protect each other, especially from you, is a big plus. For instance, if you have "pushed" or if the client feels threatened by you, you can appoint one or more "guardians" to that person to serve as protectors from you. You, of course, must give over to the "guardian." This can help someone take a risk they might not otherwise take. It also makes the group trust you more and trust and depend on each other more. Therefore, the whole environment becomes safer.

You should not let anything you have become aware of pass. If you experience the slightest incident (two people talking, someone reading a book, anything that distracts you), you should make sure it is included in the group experience. This, too, even if it turns out to be unimportant, helps to create a safe place. Along the same lines, any experience that group members have outside of the group needs to be brought back into the group. Some group leaders discourage any relationships outside of the group. I think this is a mistake because the opportunity to have the special, intimate relationships that groups can spark should not be wasted. The very process of revealing yourself and taking the other in creates an intimacy that we're all longing for in our lives. Relationships will develop in groups regardless, but will be kept private if they're discouraged. When a sexual relationship, special friendship, meeting, or phone call is kept private, it creates a schizoid-like split in the group. It's like an energy leak that makes the group unsafe. If these relationships are brought back into the group, however, the group has a chance to process very rich and meaningful material about the way each person feels about the relationship. Allowing reactions both from those "left out" and those in the relationship, without judgment, benefits the whole group.

At least ten minutes should be left at the end of every group to give people who might be holding onto something a chance to share it. This will allow them to feel better about themselves and helps to build a safe environment.

Competition and Conflict

There are two main types of competition that occur in a group.

1. Competition or conflict among the members of the group to be the favorite and get the attention of the leader.

The important thing for leaders to remember is not to try to be impartial and fair, but to allow the competition or conflict to come out and be exposed. The work is not about what will happen or who will win, but is about discovering the deep misconceptions in the soul that need to be healed. A valuable barometer is to ask those who worked whether they feel closer, more distant from each other, or the same as they did before. Also, check out whether they feel good about themselves. Knowing what makes you feel good about yourself and what makes you feel closer to others is useful because it's usually the opposite of what you think. For example, when someone expresses the lower-self quality of anger, it will usually make those involved feel closer to each other. This is because they were aware of the negative energy anyway, so the act of letting it out brings relief and safety. When reality has a chance to present itself, even if it is unpleasant or undesired, there is joy in the soul.

2. Competition or conflict with the leader to be better, know more, acquire the allegiance of the other group members, have the leader fail, and *become the leader*.

Competition with the leader is somewhat different from competition between members of the group. The task for the leader is both to accept competition and to create an environment where it's safe to compete without needing to compete in return. Admire the courage of a group member who expresses competitiveness and allow this person to feel the support of the group as much as possible. This is another example of a situation where it's easy for the group leader to hinder the development of the group. If the leader competes back, he or she will probably win the competition, but will lose a valuable opportunity to create safety and trust with this individual. If you're the leader, it's important to acknowledge the competition as soon as you become conscious of it. Once that has happened, try to create an environment that allows the person to explore it as directly as possible. Make it clear that the group will hear the issue, as everyone has a desire to know the truth. If the issue the group member brings up highlights a mistake you have made, it is wonderful to be able to say, "I'm sorry." Of course, never say, "I'm sorry" if it's not the truth. What's important is to bring the conflict out into the group's consciousness and then trust that whatever happens will be okay.

Music

I use music in all my groups. Music has the potential to create an emotional memory. When you hear a song, the emotions it triggers become wedded to your memory of the song. When you hear the song again, the same emotions surface. For instance, if at the end of every group, a certain song that touches the group members' hearts is played, it will help the members open their hearts and feel a certain bond with each other. I want to say clearly "it will help," but this doesn't mean everyone's hearts will open. Many other components must be in place before this will happen, but music can be one of these factors. Even hearing the song outside of the group will bring up feelings about the group and certain memories. There are also times when a client might be struggling with an emotion, such as sadness. A song might trigger an emotional memory and help this person cry.

Another important use of music is pleasure. Music lightens the work and allows it to be fun. Of course, we can do Core Energetic exercises to music. We can dance and create a pleasurable energy together.

Prayer

Perhaps one of the most important but forgotten tools group leaders can rely on is prayer. Prayer can be used at the beginning of a group or in the attunement. When praying, leaders might ask that they give their best or that everyone in the group get what they need.

There are also prayers during the work. Leaders can pray that clients feel good about themselves or that they take risks.

For anything to happen in a session, risk-taking is required. If everything is comfortable, nothing will happen. Clients need to be uncomfortable, disturbed. It's important to note that clients will never take risks if their practitioners don't take them. Examples of risks are saying "no," saying "yes," crying, laughing, pushing beyond one's comfort zone, and opening the heart and letting it show. Don't be afraid to pray for the ability to take these risks.

There is another kind of prayer altogether, however, and it's this kind of prayer I want to encourage you to consider more often. In this prayer, you ask to relinquish the need to know what to do. You ask to get yourself out of the way and to let God do the work while you watch. For example, you may be feeling "stuck," meaning that you don't know what to do. In my opinion, this is a good thing. If you always know what to do, you're in your head and not with God. When you're stuck, pause and allow God to take over. That means doing nothing—taking no action whatsoever. Just wait and pray for God to do it. Clients don't know you're stuck. They just feel they're patiently being sent love. The prayer might be, "Please God help me do nothing. Help me trust that You will do it." Being stuck is just a pause in the work before you move onto the next thing. It's a pause to let God do the work for you. Simply pray to God to have the patience to wait for the next thing to happen, and trust that whatever happens is sent by God. You may need to move your own energy by jumping up and down. This may help you continue to work from a centered place. The group will feel safe witnessing this behavior, because they will see your humanness. If you do something unusual, it is important to check with the group to see how they felt about it. The responses may offer the most important piece of work that day.

Finally, no matter how any group is going, during every fifth or sixth meeting, time should be allocated to work on issues between the members of the group, as opposed to group members' individual issues. Doing this will prevent slights, judgments, and so on from going underground. Having a forum where the only work done that day relates to interactions between members of the group clears the air and keeps group members feeling safe.

Interrupted Sessions

One of my favorite teaching tools is the interrupted session. It allows more of the class to participate and brings out all of the struggles and difficulties in the session. This makes the teaching more exciting and alive.

An interrupted session begins with someone volunteering to be the client and another volunteering to be the practitioner. Both need to accept their roles as real. The client must want to take a step on his or her journey, and the practitioner must genuinely want to help. Interrupting the session at certain times to point out other ways of doing something or to change where the practitioner is standing in relation to the client is a very exciting way of teaching. It keeps the teaching in the moment. The session can continue after the interruption. I always make notes about what difference the changes made and share them with the group.

Stopping the session at a certain point and having a different student in the class be the "practitioner" is another example of an interrupted session. This switch stops students from thinking they can do it better because they, in fact, get a chance to become the practitioner themselves. It also makes the class more exciting, as there's potential involvement from a number of students.

It's amazing how deep interrupted sessions can be. The degree to which one client can be helped by several different therapists is surprising. If, for some reason, the session feels incomplete, the teacher can end the session by showing students what could have been done differently.

The main thrust of Core Energetic teaching comes at the end of sessions, when students and the teacher can point out other choices that would have made the work more effective. The primary goal for student practitioners is to feel good about themselves at the end of the sessions. If they feel good about themselves, they will surely have done good work.

Chapter 8
Conclusion

I mentioned at the beginning of this book that Core Energetics was a way of life for me. Indeed, after thirty years of doing this work, I have developed tools, things I do regularly to keep me more present in life and therefore more fulfilled. I use one of these tools a few times a week, though I could benefit from using it daily. I set aside time to move my aggressive energy. I'm aware that I have cruelty and rage in me. I like to pretend that I have evolved to a higher plane and am just goodness and love, but I know that's not true. What works for me is to lie down on a mattress and kick and punch and have a temper tantrum. I then hold my legs and arms up in the air to discharge the feelings back into my body. This only takes about ten minutes and leaves me feeling more alive.

My main tool, though, is to talk to God many times a day. I don't need to have a special posture or a special place to do it. I can be in a car, on a train, or walking on the street. Something is always disturbing me, frankly, and so I ask for help. "Why did that woman look at me funny?" I might ask. "Why do I feel badly about the contact I just had with that man?" "Why do I feel lonely today?" God always answers my questions with loving answers that help me look into myself. The answers come into my head as words without sound. I don't always listen to them, however. Sometimes God tells me something to do, something I don't feel ready to do, like write a book. God told me to write this book seven years ago, but I wasn't ready. I make sure to honor how I'm feeling when I talk to God. If I always have to do what God says, I'll be afraid to ask the questions. I need to be able to say "no," so I can at least hear the wisdom.

Until I was thirty-five-years old, I didn't believe in God. There came a time in my life's journey, though, when enough had happened to make it clear that I was missing something vital. I realized praying was simply talking to God, appreciating God's gifts, and asking for help with what I didn't understand. This was when I was inspired to create and say my first prayer. Wanting to say the prayer and actually saying it were almost as important as the prayer itself. The prayer affirms the joy and excitement that life has to offer when I have the willingness to experience what is always there, but is also new every day. For this, I have Core Energetics to thank.

> **"Dear God thank you.**
> **I see things I have never seen.**
> **I hear things I have never heard.**
> **I smell things I have never smelled.**
> **And I feel things I have never felt.**
> **Dear God thank you."**

Suggested Sources and References

Web Sites:

New York Institute of Core Energetics:

www.coreenergeticseast.org

United States Association of Body Psychotherapists:
www.usabp.org

Administrative Director Core Energetics East: Joan Groom;
phone: 1-908-499-4080

Books:

John Pierrakos, Core Energetics, 1987

John Pierrakos, Eros, Love, and Sexuality, 1997

Alexander Lowen, The Betrayal of the Body, 1967

Alexander Lowen, Bioenergetics, 1975

Barbara Brennan, Hands of Light, 1987

Wilhelm Reich, Character Analysis, 1972

Wilhelm Reich, Function of the Orgasm, 1973
Journal of Energy and Consciousness, Volumes 1 to 6, 1993–98

0-595-32885-7

Printed in the United States
26483LVS00005B/385

9 780595 328857